# CONTENTS

What are the Middle Ages?                    4

Materials and methods                        6

Local traditions                             8

Symbols and stories                         10

Art for churches                            12

Romanesque churches                         14

Gothic churches                             16

Gothic glory                                18

Art for kings                               20

Beautiful books                             22

Medieval sculpture                          24

Painted pictures                            26

The end of the Middle Ages                  28

Timeline                                    30

Glossary                                    31

Places to visit                             32

Index                                       32

# WHAT ARE THE MIDDLE AGES?

The Middle Ages are the long period in Britain and Europe which begins in the centuries that led up to the **Norman** Conquest in 1066, and goes on to about 1450. The word medieval is used to describe something that comes from the Middle Ages.

## The early Middle Ages

After the fall of the **Roman Empire** in the West in the 5th century, Europe was governed by various Northern European groups (such as the Saxons) that had forced their way into southern and western Europe. Christianity had been adopted by the Romans. The Northern tribes gradually converted to Christianity but they also kept many of their own traditions and ways of life.

**Three periods of art**
Medieval art is usually divided into three main periods:
• Early Medieval, to about 1050;
• **Romanesque**, AD1050–1150;
• **Gothic**, AD1150–1400.
  Some of these periods overlap. The Early Medieval period features a mixture of Christian and Northern styles and subjects. The Romanesque period has buildings that are simple and solid, and art that is full of movement. In the Gothic period, buildings focus on height, light and colour, and art becomes more elegant and refined.

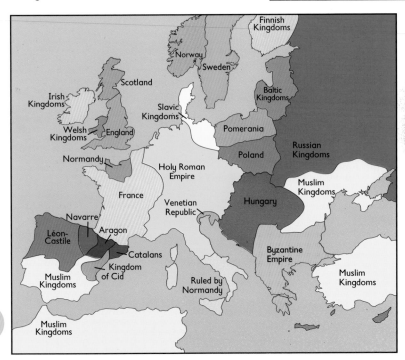

*This map shows Britain and Europe around 1100. Medieval Europe was made up of many small kingdoms and states.*

# ART OF THE MIDDLE AGES

**Jennifer Olmsted**

**Heinemann** LIBRARY

**H** www.heinemann.co.uk/library
Visit our website to find out more information about Heinemann Library books.

To order:
☎ Phone 44 (0) 1865 888066
📄 Send a fax to 44 (0) 1865 314091
💻 Visit the Heinemann Bookshop at www.heinemann.co.uk/library to browse our catalogue and order online.

First published in Great Britain by Heinemann Library, Halley Court, Jordan Hill, Oxford, OX2 8EJ, a division of Reed Educational and Professional Publishing Ltd.
Heinemann is a registered trademark of Reed Educational and Professional Publishing Ltd.

OXFORD MELBOURNE AUCKLAND
JOHANNESBURG BLANTYRE GABORONE
IBADAN PORTSMOUTH NH (USA) CHICAGO

© Reed Educational and Professional Publishing Ltd 2002
The moral right of the proprietor has been asserted.

Originated by Dot Gradations
Printed in Wing King Tong in Hong Kong.

ISBN 0 431 05589 0 (hardback)          ISBN 0 431 05594 7 (paperback)
05 04 03 02 01                                    06 05 04 03 02 01
10 9 8 7 6 5 4 3 2 1                          10 9 8 7 6 5 4 3 2 1

British Library Cataloguing in Publication Data

Olmsted, Jennifer
Art of the Middle Ages. - (Art in history)
1. Art, Medieval
I. Title
709'.02

### Acknowledgments

The author and the publisher are grateful to the following for permission to reproduce copyright photographs: © Art Resource/The Pierpont Morgan Library, p. 20; © Art Resource/Scala, p. 13; © The Bridgeman Art Library Int'l. Ltd. (U.S.)/Bibliotheque Nationale, Paris, France, p. 7; © The Bridgeman Art Library Int'l. Ltd. (U.S.)/Musee de la Tapisserie, Bayeux France/Visual Arts Library, London, p. 5; © The Bridgeman Art Library Int'l. Ltd. (U.S.)/ Cathedral of Notre Dame, Reims, France, p. 25; © The Bridgeman Art Library Int'l. Ltd. (U.S.)/Scrovegni (Arena) Chapel, Padua, Italy, p. 28; © British Library/Carpet page. Lindisfarne, p. 9; © By permission of British Museum, p. 8; © Corbis/Archivo Iconografico, S.A., p. 10; © Corbis/Dave Bartruff, p. 15; © Corbis/Bettmann, p. 11; © Corbis/Dean Conger, p. 18; © Corbis/Marc Garanger, p. 14; © Corbis/Angelo Hornak, p. 16; © Corbis/Richard List, p. 17; © Corbis/National Gallery Collection; By kind permission of the Trustees of the National Gallery, London, p. 29; © Corbis/Vanni Archive/Ruggero Vanni, pp. 12, 24; © Corbis/Gian Berto Vanni, p. 26; © The Granger Collection, p. 22; © Metropolitan Museum of Art/The Metropolitan Museum of Art, The Cloisters Collection, 1954. (54.1.2) Photograph © 1991, p. 23; © Courtesy of Niedersachsisches Landesmuseum, p. 6; © Uppsala Universitetsbibliotek/Reprosektionen, p. 21; © The Walters Art Gallery, Baltimore, p. 19.

Cover photograph reproduced with permission of Musee de la Tapisserie, Bayeux France/Visual Arts Library, London/Bridgeman Art Library.

Special thanks to Dr Kelly Holbert and Christopher Gibb for their comments in the preparation of this book.

Every effort has been made to contact copyright holders of any material reproduced in this book. Any omissions will be rectified in subsequent printings if notice is given to the publisher.

Some words are shown in bold, **like this.** You can find out what they mean by looking in the Glossary.

:NAVIGIO:

MAR E

Many of the improvements introduced under the Roman Empire were neglected – such as the extensive road network, water supply systems and farming methods. Less time and energy were spent on art and grand building schemes.

Duke William and his Fleet cross the Channel to Pevensey, *detail from the* Bayeux Tapestry, *wool embroidery on linen, height 50.8 cm length 70 m, about 1070–1080.*

*In this scene of the tapestry you can see the Norman soldiers and their horses riding in ships on their way to do battle in England.*

## The later Middle Ages

After about 1000, lords, kings and leaders of the church fought for control of the towns and farmland. The illustration on this page is from the Bayeux **tapestry**. It tells the story behind one of these battles, which took place at Hastings, and of the **Norman** conquest of England in 1066. Sometimes kings and church leaders joined forces. The **Crusades**, a series of wars that began in 1095 between the Christians of Europe and the Muslims in the Middle East, were an example of this. The Christian church became very strong, because it was the focal point of medieval life.

# MATERIALS AND METHODS

## Medieval artists

During the Middle Ages, most artists were either **monks** or **craftspeople**. Monks are men who live shut away from the world in **monasteries**, so they can pray and serve God. Craftspeople are people whose job is making beautiful objects. Until the 12th century, most people who made art were monks. Later, craftspeople took over this task. Some medieval craftspeople lived and worked in one town all their lives. Others, such as **masons** travelled from town to town. During the **Gothic** period, all craftspeople belonged to **guilds**. Guilds controlled the pricing and sale of art, and organized the training of craftspeople. The guilds also supported the families of guild members who died. Masons were craftspeople who specialized in stonework. Working with architects, they designed churches and directed the workers who built them. Many masons belonged to guilds.

Artists in the Middle Ages rarely signed their works. They made things to honour God or kings. The person who made the works of art was not important.

*Wooden panel from a choir stall showing a monk carving a choir stall, Germany, 1284.*

*The monk uses a hammer and chisel to carve a wooden seat. Other tools hang on the wall beside him.*

## Artists' materials

Medieval artists worked with many different materials. They sometimes painted on walls and wood panels, but few of these survive. More often, artists painted on treated animal skins, called **parchment** or **vellum**, which were bound into books. To make paint, artists had to grind **pigments** and then mix them with resin (a liquid made from tree sap), water, egg yolk or, more rarely, oil. Brushes were made out of animal hair or fur, that was tied to the quill of a feather or wooden stick.

Sculptors and woodworkers used stone and wood to make statues. Craftspeople made beautiful objects out of glass, ivory, enamel, gold, silver and bronze. Other kinds of artists made **tapestries**, which were painstakingly woven and sometimes richly embroidered.

### Women artists

Most artists were men, but there were women artists too. Nuns sometimes made books and paintings. Women also made tapestries and textiles.

The story of Thamyris from De Claris Mulierbus, *Giovanni Boccaccio (1313–75), from his* Book of Famous and Noble Women, *1402.*

This **illumination** shows a woman painting while her male apprentice grinds pigments.

# LOCAL TRADITIONS

### Art of early Europe

During the early Middle Ages many people made beautiful objects. As in ancient times, jewellery was one of the most common types of art. **Craftspeople** made pins, buckles, knife handles, crowns, weapons and mirrors out of gold, silver and bronze. Sometimes they added precious gems and **enamel**. Their workmanship was of a very high quality.

Some northern people, like the Vikings, made complicated wood carvings for their ships, houses, beds and other belongings. The Vikings also carved and painted stones with pictures of battles and folktales.

The **Saxons** also used a complicated pattern for decoration. It is called interlace, because it looks like ribbons twisted and woven together.

*Golden buckle of Sutton Hoo, length 13.4 cm England, about 600–700.*

*This golden belt buckle was found among the buried treasure of a Saxon king named Raedwald. He ruled before Christianity had reached all of England. The patterns in the gold are interlace patterns.*

## Local traditions and the new religion

At the same time that early **medieval** peoples made works of art, Christianity began to spread from Rome to the rest of Europe. Local art forms changed as people embraced the new religion. People in different regions took Christian **symbols**, like the cross, and added their own decorations to them. Much religious art was made with patterns and themes that came from local traditions.

This beautiful page from a book is called a 'carpet page' because it looks like an oriental carpet. The artists used a cross, the most important Christian symbol. They combined this new symbol with their own local tradition of interlace.

*Carpet page with a cross, illustration from the* Lindisfarne Gospels, *England, 34.3 cm x 23.5 cm, about 700.*

# SYMBOLS AND STORIES

## The break with tradition

In ancient Greece and Rome, people preferred art that looked very lifelike and natural. During the Middle Ages, lifelike qualities were much less important. **Medieval** art focused on the ideas behind the images. **Symbolism** and stories were very important because they helped explain these ideas. The painting on this page shows Christ on a throne. Several symbols tell us that he is Christ: the **halo** with the cross in it, the open book on his lap, his hand gesture, and the **mandorla** that surrounds him. Along with Christ's rich robes and stern expression, these symbols encouraged awe and respect.

Christ in Majesty, *wall painting from the* **apse** *of San Clemente of Tahull, Spain, about 1123.*

This image of Christ is painted on the ceiling of a church, so that people could look up during the service and remember why it was important to worship God.

Birth of Christ, *from a 12th-century manuscript in Cassel, Germany.*

This page shows the story of Christ's birth. He and his mother, Mary, both have halos to show that they are holy.

## Subjects and symbols

A great deal of medieval art was about themes from the Bible. Some art also showed the lives of saints and church leaders. Medieval artists used Christian symbols that are still used today. One important symbol in medieval art is the cross. It is the most important Christian symbol because it stands for the death and **resurrection** of Jesus Christ. The halo, another important symbol, is a sign of holiness. It is used only for images of Jesus, his family, God and the saints.

---

### Art that tells stories

Medieval artists made paintings and sculptures that told stories from the Bible. Most people in the Middle Ages could not read. Art helped them learn about God because it used pictures instead of words to tell stories. Symbols helped people understand who was in the pictures.

# ART FOR CHURCHES

Churches were very important places for art during the Middle Ages. Most art was made for churches. Church leaders, kings and noblemen hired artists to do this. One reason for having art in churches was that it was a sign of **devotion**. Spending money on expensive materials and craftsmanship showed respect and honour for God.

Another reason was that the church was a central, shared space for all members of society. Rich and poor people alike went to **Mass**. By telling stories in pictures, art taught them about Christianity. Art also persuaded people to become or remain Christians. It took a long time for Christianity to grow strong in Europe. Scenes like the one in the picture, sculpted above a **cathedral** door, showed frightening themes that encouraged people to be good Christians.

Last Judgement, by Gislebertus, above the doorway, Autun Cathedral, France, about 1120–35.

This sculpture shows Christ separating the good Christians from the bad ones, to decide who would go to Heaven.

## Celebrating Christianity

Many types of art were found in churches. Paintings appeared on the walls and ceilings of some. Often too, churches had sculptures inside and out. Sculptors carved scenes on columns, walls and portals (doorways). They also made statues of holy figures. Sculptors who specialized in wood carved seats for the clergy as well as screens that separated parts of the church from each other. Metalworkers and ivory carvers made cups called chalices, plates called patens, and crosses. These objects were especially important because they were needed for Mass.

The Altar of Saint Ambrose, *by Wolvinus, gold with enamel and gems, 80 cm x 213 cm Sant'Ambrogio, Milan, Italy, about 824–66.*

*The artist Wolvinus made this altar for an archbishop named Angilbert II, who wanted to honour Saint Ambrose. The archbishop would have used the altar for Mass.*

# ROMANESQUE CHURCHES

Many churches and **cathedrals** were built in Europe during the time known as the **Romanesque** period, from about 1050 to 1150. These churches shared some common features, which make up the Romanesque style. One was the use of rounded arches above windows and doors. These arches also appeared in the ceilings of the churches, called vaults.

Another feature of the Romanesque style was the division of the church into separate parts. This allowed several activities to take place at the same time. Like earlier churches, Romanesque churches were built in the shape of a cross. The large central space in the church, called the **nave**, allowed large numbers of church members to hear **Mass**. People prayed in small chapels in the wings of the church or cathedral. Sculptures often covered the spaces around the doorways.

*Saint Sernin, Toulouse, France, 1070–1096.*

*The cathedral of Saint Sernin was an important church. Windows with rounded arches cover the outside of the building. You can also see the small chapels that are part of the church.*

## Buildings for pilgrims

Throughout the Middle Ages, people travelled to holy sites to show their faith. These people were called pilgrims. During Romanesque times, the number of pilgrims grew very large. Pilgrims followed special routes across Europe and the Middle East to visit places where important religious events had taken place. The most famous of these in England were the shrine of St Thomas à Becket at Canterbury, and the Abbey of the Virgin Mary at Walsingham. Towns along the pilgrimage routes raised money to build huge churches which were designed to hold large numbers of people. Many were built on the most important Christian sites. They also held the **relics** of saints.

*Interior of the cathedral of Santiago de Compostela, Spain, 1075–1120.*

*This important cathedral was the destination for many pilgrims from all over Europe. It held the tomb and relics of St James.*

---

### Medieval pilgrims

In his book, *The Canterbury Tales*, the English poet Geoffrey Chaucer describes a character who had made most of the trips that pilgrims took in Romanesque and **Gothic** times:

And three times had she been at Jerusalem;
She had passed many a strange stream;
At Rome she had been, and at Bologna,
In France at St James, and at Cologne.
She knew much of wandering by the way.

---

# GOTHIC CHURCHES

The **Gothic** style in art and architecture began in France about 1150, and continued until the 15th century in some parts of Europe. Suger, the **abbot** of an important **monastery** in France, introduced many of the new ideas that led to the Gothic style in buildings. He had travelled a lot and seen many types of buildings. He worked closely with **masons** to develop new ideas. Saint Denis, the **abbey** church he helped build in northern France, was the first Gothic church in Europe.

## Space and light

In the Gothic period, the heavy pillars of the **Romanesque** style were no longer used. Instead, masons used new supports called **buttresses** that held up the walls from the outside of the church. Masons used buttresses to build high, thin walls that made the churches seem open and airy inside. The sense of space was emphasized by huge stained-glass windows that let in light. Inside, masons drew attention to the height of the church with tall, thin columns that ran from floor to ceiling. In Britain, flying buttresses allowed masons to build **cathedrals** with tall towers and spires, such as those of Salisbury.

**Nave,** *Amiens Cathedral, 1220–88, France, 42 m high.*

*Masons used tall, thin columns and ceilings with pointed arches to make the church seem even taller than it was. Beautiful stained-glass windows let in light and colour.*

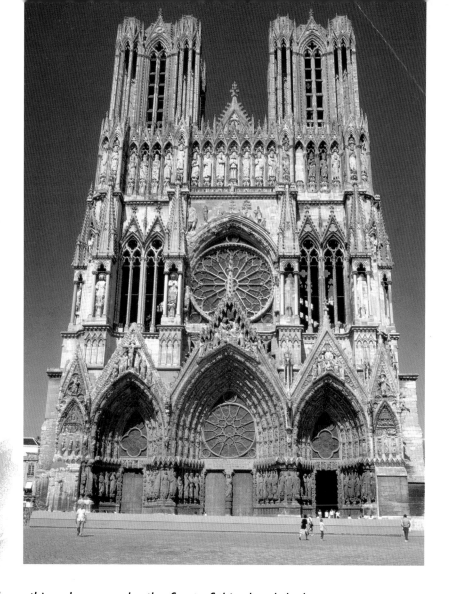

West side, Reims Cathedral, France, 1220–60, towers mid-15th century.

*Pointed arches and long, thin columns make the front of this church look very impressive. The huge round window at the front, called a rose window, fills the inside with coloured light. There are hundreds of sculptures on the front of this church.*

Another key feature of Gothic churches was the pointed arch above doors and windows on the outside of the church. The shape and slenderness of the arch drew your eye upwards. These arches also emphasized the height of the church. Gothic masons stressed height inside and outside because many people thought of the church as the house of God, who lived up in the heavens. To make them even more beautiful, Gothic sculptors covered the fronts of churches with statues. The cathedrals of Wells and Lincoln in England are two wonderful examples of this.

# GOTHIC GLORY

**Buttresses** allowed **Gothic masons** to put large windows in church walls. The windows were made of stained glass. These beautiful windows filled the churches with colour and light. The windows also had pictures that told stories.

## How stained glass was made

First the metal outlines that held the glass were made. Then craftspeople mixed **pigments** with sand and other glass-making materials, and heated them until they melted together. After the sheet of coloured glass cooled, they cut it into small pieces. Each sheet was one colour, so many different sheets were made. The small pieces of glass were placed in their proper places in the metal frame. Then everything was heated again to seal the glass to the metal.

*Christ entering Jerusalem, stained-glass window, west side of Chartres Cathedral, France, about 1200–36.*

*This image is part of a window that illustrates the story of Christ's life. There are more than 100 stained-glass windows in Chartres Cathedral.*

Attack on the Castle of Love, *lid from a jewellery casket, ivory with iron mounts, about 1330–50.*

*The two central panels show two knights jousting while their ladies watch from the balcony. All the panels show themes that refer to love.*

## Ivory carving

Ivory carving was common throughout the Middle Ages, but it reached a new height during the Gothic period. Ivory, taken from the tusks of elephants, was a highly prized material. It was used to make **devotional** sculptures and **secular** objects like the **casket** on this page. Ivory is a hard material, but it can be carved with sharp metal tools. It was carved into three-dimensional statues and into reliefs – pictures carved to stand out from a stone, wood or ivory background. Skilled artists could add many tiny details, such as fluttering flags or braided hair.

**Using ivory**

Small ivory panels with relief carvings were used on book covers, **reliquaries**, statues, and **crucifixes**. During the Gothic period, ivory was also used to make luxury items, including mirror cases, combs and caskets for jewellery. The theme of the scenes on these objects was usually love.

# ART FOR KINGS

Kings and other rulers had sculpture, **tapestries**, robes, crowns and other kinds of art and crafts made for them. They preferred works of art that showed their power and their right to rule. There were many ways to do this. Many kings built huge palaces or castles and filled them with beautiful tapestries, books, and gold and silver objects. Another way of showing their strength as leaders was to pay for works of art that told stories of their military successes. Some of these works were displayed in the courts, while some were put into books for later rulers to see.

Kings also showed their power by buying things made out of expensive materials. Gold crowns studded with precious gems are one example.

Kings, queens and other leaders often wore robes made out of silk, fur and other rich materials. Ordinary people were not allowed to wear such things, and could not afford them anyway.

Blanche of Castile and King Louis IX of France, *page from a French* Moralized Bible, *about. 1230.*

*The wealth and power of the king of France and his mother are shown here by the rich colours of their clothing, and by the gold background of the page.*

# Kings and the church

Another way for kings to show their power was to buy art for churches. This showed the kings' **devotion** to God. It also showed off their wealth.

Many kings defended their right to rule by saying that God or Jesus approved of their leadership. For much of the Middle Ages, French kings were crowned and buried in the same two churches. This was to show the people of France that God approved of the king's right to rule, and approved of the way the king had lived his life. Some kings also paid for works of art that showed God crowning them. This was not meant to be seen as a real event. Instead, it was a **symbol** of the king's right to rule.

Christ Crowning the Emperor Henry III and the Empress Agnes, from the Uppsala Gospels, Echternach, Germany, completed in 1050.

The powerful German emperor Henry III gave this book to the cathedral at Goslar. The painting shown here suggests that Jesus himself gave Henry the right to rule.

# BEAUTIFUL BOOKS

In the Middle Ages, books were made by hand. Until the **Gothic** period, most books were made in **monasteries**. At first, only **monks** made books. During the Gothic period **universities** were built, and they began to replace monasteries as places for learning. **Secular** artists joined the monks in making books at this time, and eventually they took over the art of book-making. At the very end of the Middle Ages, printed books were invented.

## How books were made

Instead of paper, **medieval** books were made of sheets of **parchment** or **vellum**. Both these materials were made from animal skins that had been scraped until they were very thin. Scribes used ink to copy texts from older books. Then artists called **illuminators** painted small, brightly coloured illustrations, called **illuminations,** in these copies. The illumination on this page shows a scribe and an illuminator at work. More expensive books had another step, where gold was added to the illuminations. The whole process required careful planning, expensive materials and a lot of time.

*A scribe and illuminator in the monastery at Echternach, Pericope Book, Germany, mid–eleventh century.*

*The clothing of these men shows that the scribe is a secular artist and the illuminator is a monk.*

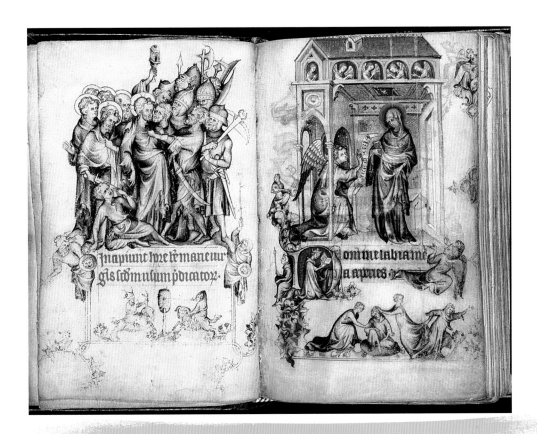

*Illuminations from* The Hours of Jeanne d'Evreux, *by Jean Pucelle, each page 9 cm x 6 cm, about 1325–28.*

*The illuminator who illustrated this book was very famous. He added fanciful scenes around the edges of the pages. If you look closely at the initial N, you can see that the queen of France is shown inside the letter, reading.*

## Audiences for books

Illustrated books were luxury items during the Middle Ages. At first, books were only available to churches, monasteries and royalty. These books contained stories from the Bible and other religious texts. Books that were made for churches were used during **Mass**. Monks, nuns and royalty used smaller books for personal prayer and **devotion.**

Later in the Middle Ages, noblemen and women were able to buy small books for personal use. The queen of France used the book shown on this page during her daily prayers. As more people learned to read, and the universities grew, there was greater demand for books. From about 1200, secular texts, including history, poetry and stories, became common.

# MEDIEVAL SCULPTURE

When making a sculpture, first the sculptor chose a block of stone or wood. He used an **adze** to remove large pieces of material, leaving a rough outline of the shape. Next, the sculptor used a chisel to carve the surface until the sculpture was nearly done. Finally, he used special drills and tools to polish parts of the sculpture and add tiny details.

## Romanesque sculpture

In **Romanesque** sculpture, monsters, animals, plants and geometric designs are common features. People of all types appear regularly. Romanesque sculpture often shows scenes from stories that were cleverly designed to fit their architectural space. People and animals were shown in lively poses, creating a feeling of movement and emotion

The Romanesque period was also the first time that carved portals (doorways) appeared in churches. These sculptures were very complex. They could include stories from the Bible, the signs of the zodiac or symbols representing the twelve months.

*Prophet and lions, south portal, Saint Pierre, Moissac, France, about 1115–30.*

*Here, you see that the sculptor carefully carved matching pairs of lions to fit in the space of the door post. The sculptor also created a feeling of movement by making the lions lean forward.*

# Gothic sculpture

Portal sculpture continued to be popular in the **Gothic** period, but there was a greater sense of order. The people in Gothic sculpture are less crowded in their settings. The figures are more three-dimensional, and look more like real people than the people in Romanesque sculpture.

During the Gothic period, wealthy people began to buy more sculptures. They preferred small sculptures, especially statues of religious figures like the Virgin Mary. They put these in their homes or gave them to churches.

Annunciation and Visitation, *centre portal, west side, Reims Cathedral, France, about. 1225–45.*

*The four figures look very calm and relaxed. You can tell that they are Gothic sculptures because they look very lifelike.*

# PAINTED PICTURES

During the Middle Ages, most people could not read. Painting pictures was important as a means of telling stories, as well as for decoration. One kind of painting that was especially important was the **illuminations** created to illustrate books. Painting on walls was also popular. Many of these paintings were **frescoes**. Frescoes are pictures that are painted on walls while the plaster on the wall is still damp. The **pigments** in the paint bind to the plaster as it dries.

Unfortunately, most of the wall paintings from the Middle Ages have not survived. Only a few are left. We know about others from drawings and descriptions in books. Like most other art in the Middle Ages, wall paintings portrayed religious subjects.

Painting on wood panels was another type of painting done in the Middle Ages, but initially it was not very common. At the end of the Middle Ages, though, it became more popular. Painted wooden panels were often found in churches behind the altar. Altar panels usually featured one holy person or a saint in the centre, with smaller story-telling scenes on the sides.

Artists used tempera, a mixture of egg yolk and pigment, for these panels. At the end of the Middle Ages, artists in the Netherlands and Germany began using oil mixed with pigment for their paints. This type of oil paint made the surface of the painting look very rich and shiny.

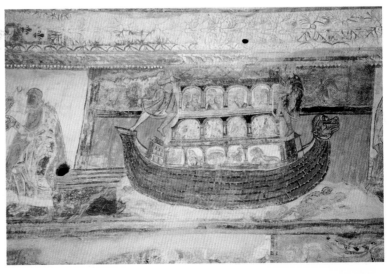

*Noah's Ark, fresco from the ceiling of the church of Saint-Savin-sur-Gartempe, France, about 1100.*

*This fresco shows a scene from the biblical story of Noah. You can see the pairs of animals in the windows of the ark.*

# Make a model medieval fresco

**You will need:**

cardboard
paper and pencil
string and scissors
poster paints
ruler and sticky tape

fine paint brush
cutting mat
plaster
craft knife

1 Sketch a design on scrap paper.
Measure the design and make a
cardboard tray the same size, with sides
5 cm deep. Score the sides, turn them
up, and tape them together.

2 Mix the plaster in an old container,
according to the instructions on the
package. Pour it into the cardboard tray
to a depth of 3 cm. Smooth the surface
of the plaster. Cut a 15 cm piece of
string and push the ends into the
wet plaster leaving a loop to hang
the finished fresco.

3 When the plaster is dry, remove it from
the tray. Trace your design onto the
smooth, bottom surface. Pencil in the
outline of your design. Apply a thin coat
of wet plaster over the top. You should
still be able to see the outline. Colour in
your design with the poster paints
while the plaster topcoat is still damp.

4 When your fresco is dry, hang it up,
using the string loop.

# THE END OF THE MIDDLE AGES

During the 14th century, the way people thought about their world and their lives began to change. These changes led to a new period called the **Renaissance**. One of the key changes was that people became more interested in the uniqueness of human beings – their individuality.

## A time of change

In the Middle Ages, a person was seen as a member of a group rather than an individual. In the Renaissance, it was believed that each person was unique. People also believed that human beings were the most special part of God's creation. Because of these changes, there was more interest in advancements people could make in science, medicine and the arts.

Joachim Among the Shepherds, *by Giotto, fresco, about 1305, Scrovegni (Arena) Chapel, Padua, Italy. 200 cm x 185 cm.*

*Giotto painted many different human emotions. Here he shows Joachim looking sad, while the shepherds look shy and uncomfortable. This picture is a good example of the way art looked at the end of the Middle Ages, since it shows both the new interest in lifelike painting and the old tradition of using a painting to portray stories from the Bible.*

## Transformations in art

The end of the Middle Ages was a time of **prosperity** in many countries. A new middle class developed, because of new trade and ways of doing business, and its members had money to spend on art. This was different from the early Middle Ages, when only church people, kings and noblemen had enough money to buy art.

People who bought art, called patrons, became more interested in subjects that showed human feelings and activities. There was also a greater desire for art that looked more lifelike. This was related to the new interest in the lifelike and natural-looking art of ancient Greece and Rome that was also part of the Renaissance.

The status of artists also changed. During the early Middle Ages, artists were usually anonymous members of **guilds** or **monasteries**. In the Renaissance, the individual styles and personalities of artists became more and more important.

*Saint Jerome in His Study, by Antonello da Messina, oil on panel, Italy, about 1450–55, 46 cm x 36 cm.*

*Antonello used new artistic techniques to make this painting look very lifelike. He used perspective to make it look as though you could walk right into this room. Perspective is a drawing technique taken from the ancient science of geometry. He also included details of everyday life to show the saint's human qualities. If you look closely at the painting you can see that he also included a lion, the **symbol** of St Jerome.*

# TIMELINE

**AD**

| | |
|---|---|
| 313 | The Roman Empire makes Christianity its official religion |
| 410 | The city of Rome is sacked. The Roman Empire crumbles in the West. |
| 596 | St Augustine is sent by Pope Gregory I to convert the English |
| about 1050 | The Romanesque period begins |
| 1066 | William the Conqueror, a Norman, conquers England |
| 1070–96 | Cathedral of Saint Sernin is built in France |
| 1075–1120 | Cathedral of Santiago de Compostela is built in Spain |
| 1081 | Ely Cathedral built |
| 1095–99 | The First Crusade to the Holy Land takes place |
| 1122 | Suger becomes Abbot of Saint Denis in France |
| 1135 | Work begins on the Abbey Church of Saint Denis, France |
| 1147–48 | The Second Crusade takes place |
| about 1150 | The Gothic period begins |
| 1175 | The rebuilding of Canterbury Cathedral in the Gothic style begins |
| 1189–93 | The Third Crusade takes place |
| 1180 | Wells Cathedral built – high point of Gothic style in west of England |
| 1192 | Lincoln Cathedral rebuilt after an earthquake |
| 1200–36 | Chartres Cathedral built in France |
| 1202–04 | The Fourth Crusade takes place |
| 1211–1311 | Reims Cathedral is built in France |
| 1220–70 | Amiens Cathedral is built in France |
| 1226 | Salisbury Cathedral built on new site in Gothic style |
| 1245 | The rebuilding of Westminster Cathedral in the Gothic style begins |
| about 1306 | Giotto paints the Scrovegni (Arena) Chapel in Italy |
| 1446 | Kings College Chapel, Cambridge built |
| about 1450 | The Renaissance begins |

# GLOSSARY

**abbey** religious centre, usually with a church and monastery

**abbot** head of a monastery

**adze** cutting tool used for trimming pieces of stone or wood from a sculpture

**apse** semicircular east end of a church, where the altar is

**buttress** sturdy stone support on the outside of a structure that holds up walls

**casket** small box that holds valuable objects

**cathedral** main church in a district

**crucifix** sculpture or painting of Jesus on the cross

**craftsperson** skilled person who makes crafts or art for a career, for example a wood carver or goldsmith

**Crusades** wars waged by Christian Europeans against Muslims in the Middle East

**devotion** related to prayer or religious feelings

**enamel** coloured liquid that becomes smooth, shiny and hard when heated

**fresco** painting made on a wall while the plaster is still damp

**Gothic** period in art that lasted from about 1150 to about 1400

**guild** group of craftspeople. Organization that controlled the sale and pricing of art, and trained craftsmen.

**halo** in painting, a circle of light around the head of a saint or holy person

**illumination** small painting in a book

**illuminator** artist or craftsman who specializes in painting illuminations

**mandorla** almond-shaped halo that goes around the whole body of an important holy person, usually Jesus

**mason** stoneworker who designed buildings and directed the workers who built them

**Mass** religious service in the Catholic church

**medieval** word used to describe something from the Middle Ages

**monastery** group of buildings, including a church, where monks live

**monk** man who devotes his life to religion. A woman who does this is called a nun.

**nave** long, central aisle of a church that leads to the altar

**Norman** member of a group of people who settled in what is now Normandy, in France

**parchment** thin, paper-like sheets made from animal hides that have been scraped, treated and trimmed

**pigment** coloured material taken from animals, plants, earth or rocks and used to make paint or dye

**prosperity** wealth and success

**relic** remains of a holy person or saint

**reliquary** special container for relics, usually made of expensive materials

**resurrection** rebirth. In Christianity it refers to Christ coming back to life after the crucifixion.

**Renaissance** period from about 1400 when people looked beyond the closed medieval world, and developed a renewed interest in Greek and Roman ideas

**Roman Empire** the Romans ruled over many lands, including Britain, most of Europe and parts of Africa for about 800 years (510 – AD410)

**Romanesque** period in art and architecture that lasted from about 1050 to 1150

**Saxon** member of a group of people from what is now Germany

**secular** something not part of or related to the church

**symbol** an object or a sign that stands for something else

**tapestry** textile with woven pictures

**university** school that taught young men about the sciences, the church and the history of thought

**vellum** paper-like material made from calfskin, like parchment, but softer and lighter

# PLACES TO VISIT

Any of Britain's great cathedrals, such as:

Canterbury Cathedral, www.canterbury-cathedral.org.uk
Lincoln Cathedral, www.lincoln-cathedral.org.uk
Westminster Cathedral, London, www.westminstercathedral.org.uk

The medieval section of the British Museum, London
Windsor Castle
The Tower of London

# INDEX

books 9, 11, 20, 20, 21, 22–23, 26
buttresses 16, 18

Canterbury Cathedral 15
cathedrals 12, 14, 15, 16, 17, 18, 25
Christianity 4, 9, 11, 12, 13,
churches 5, 6, 10, 12–13, 14–15, 16–17, 18, 21, 23, 24, 26, 27
craftsmen 6, 7, 8, 18

fresco 10, 26, 28

Gothic art 4, 6, 7, 16–17, 18–19, 20, 22, 23, 26, 2
guilds 6, 29

illuminations 6, 8, 11, 20, 21, 22–23
illuminators 22, 23
interlace 8, 9
ivory 7, 13, 19

jewellery 8, 20

kings 5, 8, 20–21

Lincoln Cathedral 17

masons 6, 16, 17, 18
monasteries 6, 16, 22, 23
monks 6, 22

Norman 5

painting 7, 9, 10, 11, 13, 20, 21, 22, 23, 26–27, 28, 29
pigments 7, 18, 26, 27
pilgrims 15

Renaissance 28, 29
Roman Empire 4
Romanesque art 4, 10, 12, 13, 14–15, 24, 26

saints 11, 13, 15, 29
Salisbury Cathedral 16
Saxon 8
scribes 22
sculptors 7, 13, 17, 24
sculpture 6, 12, 14, 17, 24–25
stained glass 18
symbolism 10–11
symbols 9, 10, 11, 21

tapestry 5, 7, 20

university 22, 23

Wells Cathedral 17

Vikings 8